*For Étienne, Émile, Léonie*
*V. A.*

*To Joséphine and Jean*
*E. T.*

Franklin Watts
First published in Great Britain in 2016 by The Watts Publishing Group

Original title: INVENTAIRE ILLUSTRÉ DE LA MER
© 2011 Albin Michel Jeunesse
Copyright English translation © The Watts Publishing Group, 2016

We would like to thank Aquarium La Rochelle SAS, education services (www.aquarium-larochelle.com) for their expert advice.

Credits

Graphics and production: cedricramadier.com
Translation: PS Translations
Editorial for this edition: Rachel Cooke
Design for this edition: Peter Scoulding

All rights reserved.

ISBN  978 1 4451 5127 4

Printed in China.

FSC
www.fsc.org

MIX
Paper from
responsible sources
FSC® C104740

Franklin Watts
An imprint of
Hachette Children's Group
Part of The Watts Publishing Group
Carmelite House
50 Victoria Embankment
London EC4Y 0DZ

An Hachette UK Company
www.hachette.co.uk

www.franklinwatts.co.uk

# Illustrated
# COMPENDIUM
## of THE SEA

Virginie
Aladjidi

Emmanuelle
Tchoukriel

# W
## FRANKLIN WATTS
### LONDON•SYDNEY

# INTRODUCTION

Welcome to this *Illustrated Compendium of the Sea*. Emmanuelle Tchoukriel is a painter-illustrator trained in medical and scientific illustration. She has drawn the marine life in this book with the precision and skill of the naturalist explorers of previous centuries. At that time, artwork was printed in books using stone or metal plates to beautiful effect. Emmanuelle has called her illustrations "plates" as well. She used a rotring nib and Indian ink to draw the black outlines, and coloured them using watercolours, which sometimes give a translucent effect. A keen diver herself, Emmanuelle has seen a number of the animals or plants featured in this book through her diving mask.

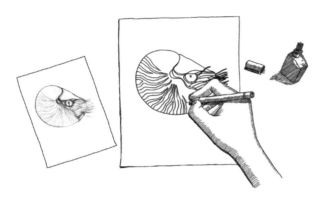 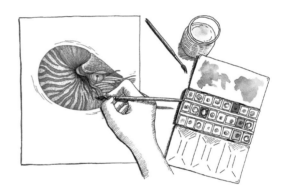

In this book, we have chosen a hundred marine species. It is far from complete. The 2010 "Census of Marine Life", a study which took over ten years to complete, listed over 250,000 marine species. Researchers claim that there are still 750,000 species to be discovered within this ecosystem – perhaps not surprising since the seas and oceans cover 70 per cent of the surface of our planet.

But marine life is threatened by overfishing, pollution and the loss of habitats. Climate change is also affecting the variety of life in our seas and oceans. More than a third of ocean species are endangered, including many featured in this book, such as the blue whale, the dugong, the green sea turtle, coral, the sawfish and the hammerhead shark.

In this book we have grouped living things using the science of classification. Living things are divided into kingdoms, including animals and plants. These groups are then divided again into phyla (singular phylum), then classes, sometimes with a subphylum in between, with further divisions down to species. But classifications change as new discoveries are made, and scientists do not always agree about how a life form should be grouped. For example, crustacea (crustaceans) used to be viewed as a class but are now more often said to be a subphylum, while mollusca (molluscs) are generally now considered a phylum.

*Virginie Aladjidi*

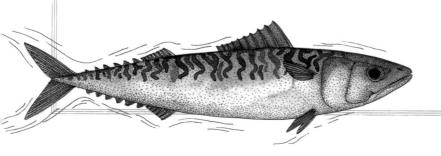

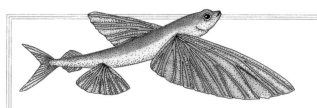

# CONTENTS

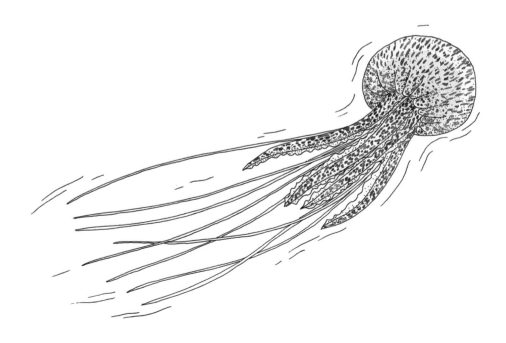

# Narwhal,
## sometimes known as the "unicorn of the sea"

*Monodon monoceros*

Class: MAMMAL

This agile whale can measure up to 5 m, excluding its famous unicorn-like horn. In fact, the horn is a long twisted tooth, which usually only the male grows. It can be over 3 m in length with around 10 million nerve endings inside it so it is probably used to detect things in the water. The narwhal has no dorsal fin, so it can swim under the ice of the Arctic Ocean, close to the North Pole. Like all marine mammals, it has to come to the surface of the water to breathe from time to time.

*— plate 1 —*

## Walrus

*Odobenus rosmarus*

Class: MAMMAL

This moustached carnivore lives in large colonies of up to a thousand animals on the pack ice of the Arctic Ocean. Its tusks are elongated canine teeth and can grow up to a metre long. Males sometimes fight with their tusks but these giant teeth also make useful ice picks!

— *plate 2* —

— *plate 3* —

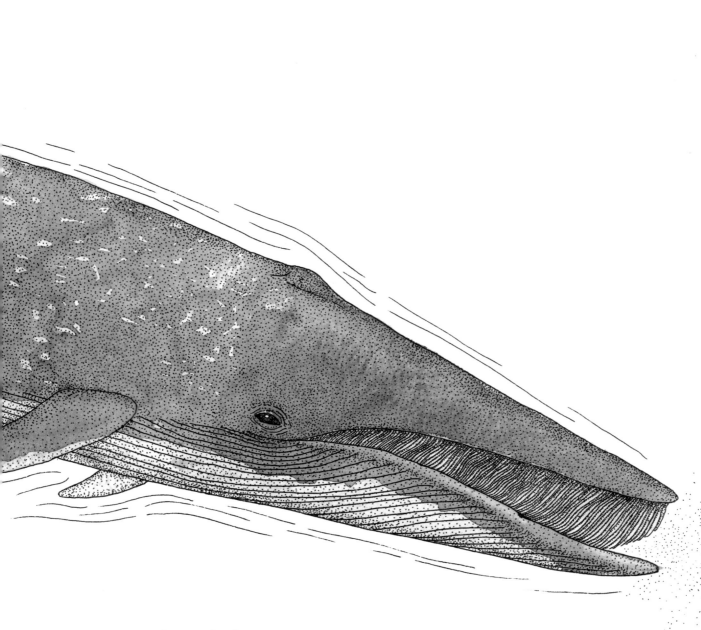

# Blue whale

*Balaenoptera musculus*

Class: MAMMAL

The long, elegant blue whale is the largest
animal ever known to have lived – bigger than
any dinosaur. It can reach up to 33 m in length
and weigh up to 173 tonnes. It swims mainly
in deep water, with its blowhole closed, but
comes up to the surface to breathe. It then
blows out a jet of water 6 to 9 m high. It lives
off krill (tiny crustaceans) which it sieves from
the water with the baleen plates that hang from
the top of its mouth.

## Brown fur seal

*Arctocephalus pusillus*

Class: MAMMAL

An excellent swimmer from around the coasts of South Africa and Australia, this seal feeds on fish out at sea and, using its back fins, pulls itself onto rocks to rest and breed. It may catch birds there as well. Unlike most other types of seal, fur seals have external ear flaps (pinnae), a characteristic they share with sea lions.

— *plate 4* —

# Dugong

*Dugong dugon*

Class: MAMMAL

The dugong is a herbivore, grazing on up
to 40 kg of seagrass a day, so it is sometimes
called a sea cow. It swims in the shallows
along the coasts of the Indian and Pacific
oceans. It measures between 3 and 4 m in
length and has a flat, triangular tail (like
a dolphin's) which distinguishes it from a
manatee, another type of sea cow.

— *plate 5* —

# Orca

*Orcinus orca*

Class: MAMMAL

The orca, often called the killer whale, is the largest member of the ocean dolphin family, with teeth and a large dorsal fin. Orcas live in family groups called pods, which hunt effectively together as a pack, preying on fish, seals, penguins and whale calves. This black and white hunter will sometimes even use waves to come briefly out of the water to grab its prey off the beach.

— *plate 6* —

## Spinner dolphin

*Stenella longirostris*

Class: MAMMAL

This small, tropical dolphin lives in groups of 20 to 100 animals feeding on small fish and squid. They are famous for their acrobatics — a dolphin may spin as much as 5.5 times in one leap out of the water. People like to watch dolphins but boats can cause stress if they get too close.

— *plate 7* —

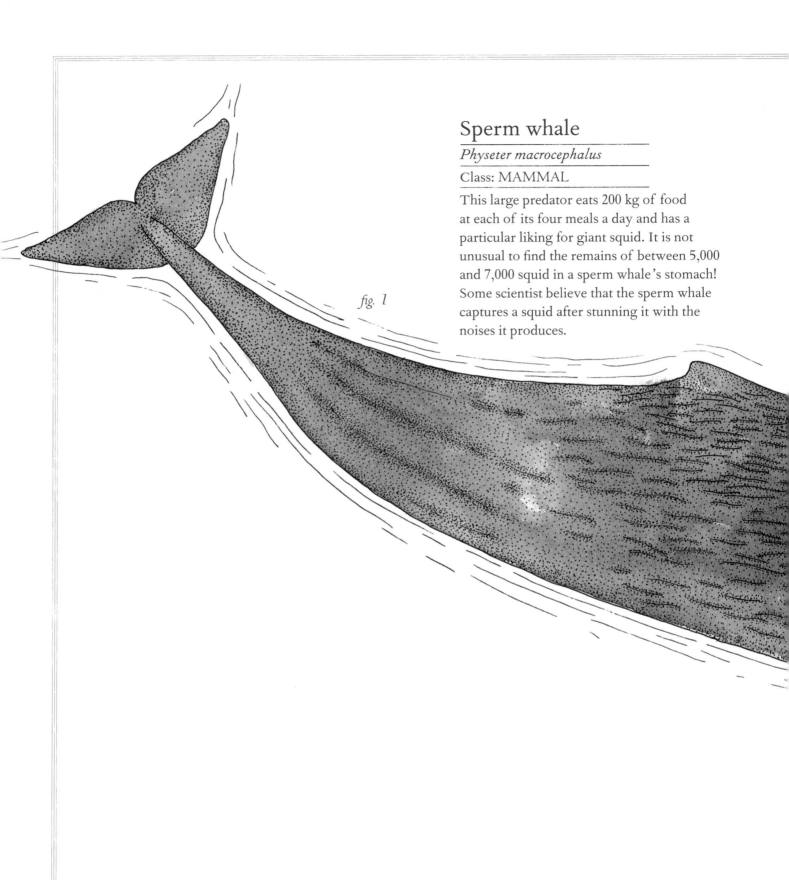

# Sperm whale

*Physeter macrocephalus*

Class: MAMMAL

This large predator eats 200 kg of food at each of its four meals a day and has a particular liking for giant squid. It is not unusual to find the remains of between 5,000 and 7,000 squid in a sperm whale's stomach! Some scientist believe that the sperm whale captures a squid after stunning it with the noises it produces.

*fig. 1*

— *plate 8* —

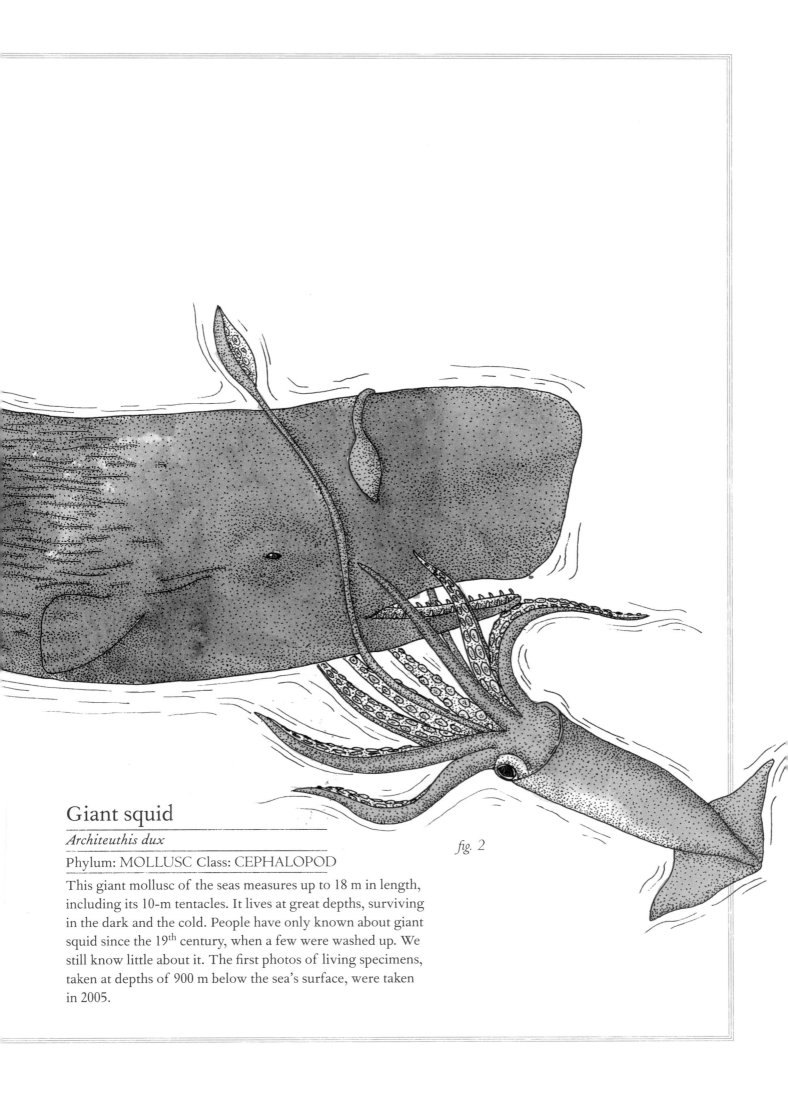

# Giant squid

*Architeuthis dux*

Phylum: MOLLUSC Class: CEPHALOPOD

This giant mollusc of the seas measures up to 18 m in length, including its 10-m tentacles. It lives at great depths, surviving in the dark and the cold. People have only known about giant squid since the 19th century, when a few were washed up. We still know little about it. The first photos of living specimens, taken at depths of 900 m below the sea's surface, were taken in 2005.

*fig. 2*

# Common octopus

*Octopus vulgaris*

Phylum: MOLLUSC Class: CEPHALOPOD

An octopus has eight tentacles, each covered with more than 200 suction cups. Using its horned jaws in the shape of a beak, the octopus grinds down shellfish that it eats. Usually an octopus crawls along the sea bed but sometimes swims through the sea by expelling water through a siphon, throwing out a cloud of ink to camouflage itself. The octopus shows intelligence rarely seen in invertebrates: it is capable of memorising and learning! It has been known to open lobster pots.

— *plate 9* —

# Common cuttlefish

*Sepia officinalis*

Phylum: MOLLUSC
Class: CEPHALOPOD

A cuttlefish has ten tentacles of which two are used to seize its prey. Unlike any other molluscs, a cuttlefish has an internal shell, commonly known as "cuttlebone", that you sometimes find washed up on the beach.

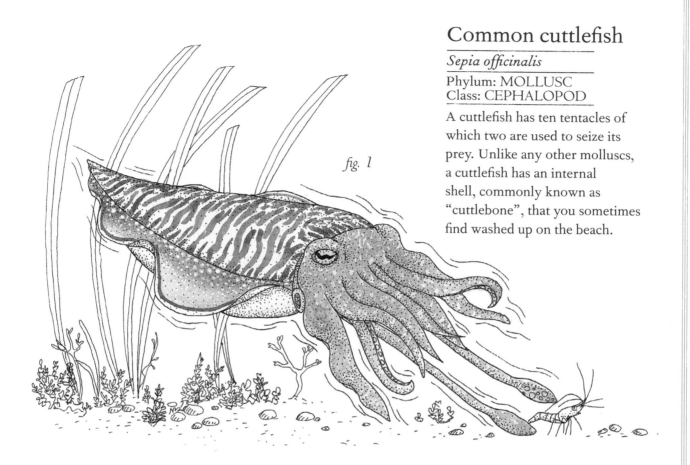

*fig. 1*

# Chambered nautilus

*Nautilus pompilius*

Phylum: MOLLUSC
Class: CEPHALOPOD

The 20-cm nautilus has existed on Earth for over 400 million years (long before the dinosaurs)! It is found close to the Pacific islands and off the coast of Australia. It is the only cephalopod with an external shell, which is made up of chambers. As the animal grows, it makes a new chamber to move into and seals off the old one, gradually forming a spiral. Its 90 tentacles (without suction cups) stick out of the last chamber.

*fig. 2*

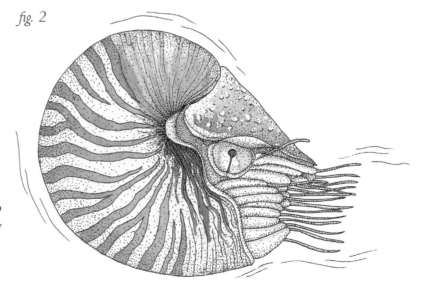

— *plate 10* —

Gastropods are a large class of mollusc with a flattened foot that they use to move forward. Commonly identified as slugs and snails on land, there are large numbers of marine gastropods as well.

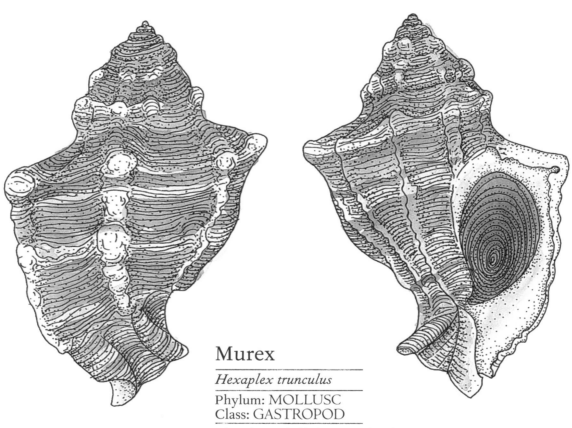

## Murex

*Hexaplex trunculus*

Phylum: MOLLUSC
Class: GASTROPOD

This thick-shelled sea snail is found around Mediterranean coasts. It has a gland that produces a purplish-violet-red mucus to clean out its shell. In ancient times, people used this mucus to make a greatly prized dye that was used to create beautiful, deep blue cloth.

— *plate 11* —

# Cowries

Phylum: MOLLUSC Class: GASTROPOD

Cowries are gastropods with a thick, shiny shell, with a toothed opening and varying designs. In the past, people have sometimes used cowrie shells as a type of money.

*fig. 1*

### Ring cowrie
*Monetaria annulus*

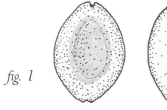

*fig. 2*

### Spotted cowrie
*Trivia monacha*

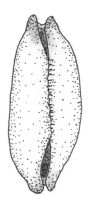

*fig. 3*

### Isabel's cowrie
*Cypraea isabella*

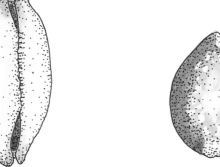

*fig. 4*

### Serpent's head cowrie
*Cypraea caputserpentis*

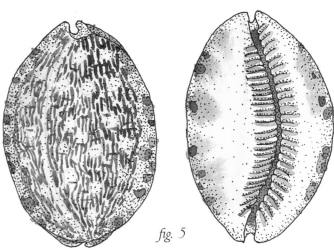

*fig. 5*

### Arabian cowrie
*Cypraea arabica*

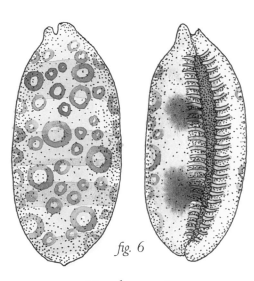

*fig. 6*

### Eyed cowrie
*Cypraea argus*

— *plate 12* —

## Common mussel

*Mytilus edulis*

Phylum: MOLLUSC Class: BIVALVE

Like all bivalves, a mussel has a two-part shell which it opens to feed on plankton in the water. Mussels live along coastlines, attached to rocks or other surfaces by their sticky "beards". They keep their shells tightly shut when the tide goes down.

*fig. 1*

*fig. 2*

## Pacific oyster

*Crassostrea gigas*

Phylum: MOLLUSC
Class: BIVALVE

This rough-shelled bivalve feeds on plankton. Originally from Japan, it is now farmed around the world.

— *plate 13* —

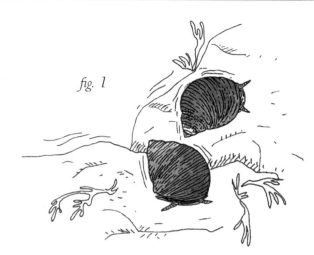

fig. 1

## Winkle

*Littorina littorea*

Phylum: MOLLUSC
Class: GASTROPOD

Winkles are small sea snails and were once a popular food at the seaside in Britain. They were often sold with whelks.

## Common whelk

*Buccinum undatum*

Phylum: MOLLUSC
Class: GASTROPOD

The large sea snail is found in the shallow waters of the Atlantic coasts.

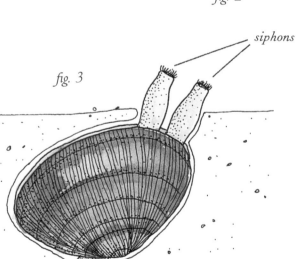

fig. 2

siphons

fig. 3

fig. 4

## Pod razor clam

*Ensis siliqua*

Phylum: MOLLUSC
Class: BIVALVE

The pod razor lives in the sand. It can bury itself as deep as 1 m using its wriggly foot.

## European clam

*Tapes decussata*

Phylum: MOLLUSC Class: BIVALVE

This bivalve has a fine-ridged shell and lives buried in the sand. The clam has two siphons: one that draws in the water and the plankton it eats, and one that expels the filtered water.

foot

— plate 14 —

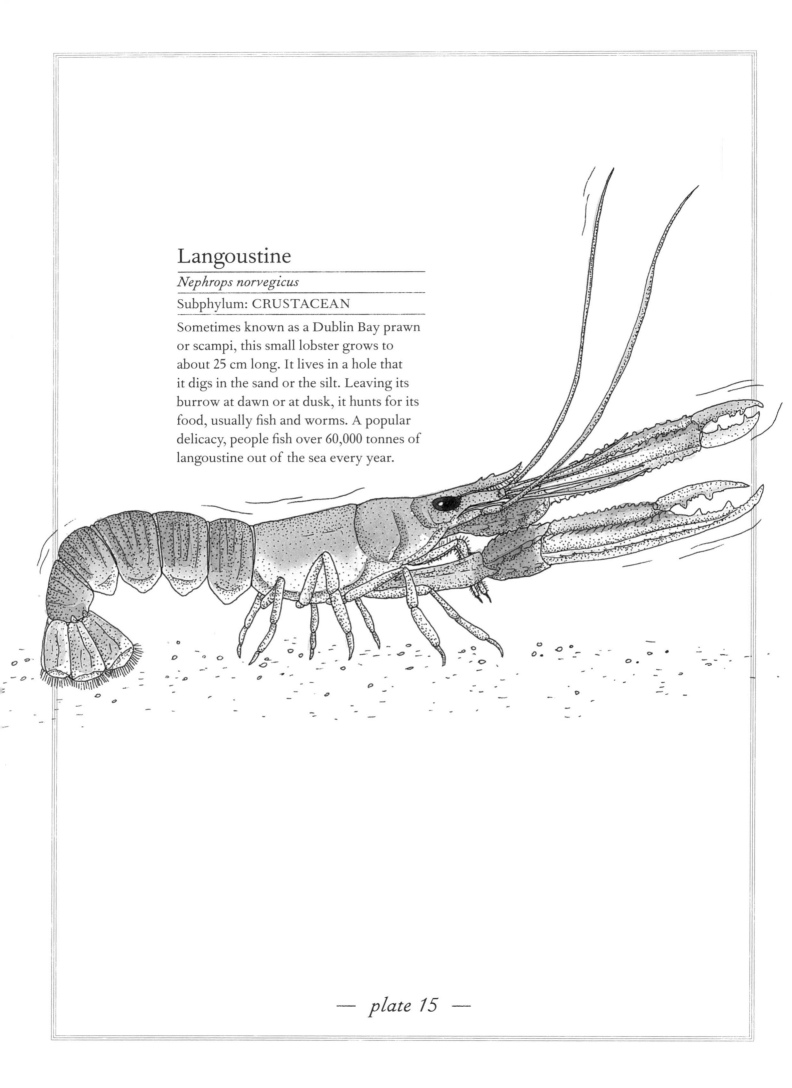

# Langoustine

*Nephrops norvegicus*

Subphylum: CRUSTACEAN

Sometimes known as a Dublin Bay prawn or scampi, this small lobster grows to about 25 cm long. It lives in a hole that it digs in the sand or the silt. Leaving its burrow at dawn or at dusk, it hunts for its food, usually fish and worms. A popular delicacy, people fish over 60,000 tonnes of langoustine out of the sea every year.

— *plate 15* —

## Acorn barnacle

*Balanus crenatus*

Subphylum: CRUSTACEAN

These crustaceans attach themselves to rocks and other animals as well, such as turtles or whales. In order to feed, they partly open the chalky plates of their shells and push out their legs to catch plankton. They close up their shells at low tide.

*fig. 1*

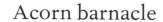

*fig. 2*

## Sea slater
(or sea roach)

*Ligia oceanica*

Subphylum: CRUSTACEAN

A relative of the woodlouse, the sea slater is found on rocky coastlines, never very far from water. These creatures can live in soils with high concentrations of salt, which make them well adapted to their seaside habitat.

— *plate 16* —

# Crustaceans and zoo plankton

Zoo plankton is made up of a whole variety of microscopic crustaceans, animal larvae (the early stage of some animals' life cycle) and also fry (young fish) that float around the sea. Zoo plankton feeds on phytoplankton, microscopic algae, or other zoo plankton. The whale shark and baleen whales feed exclusively on zoo plankton. Here are some types of crustaceans found in zoo plankton.

*fig. 1*
Crab larvae

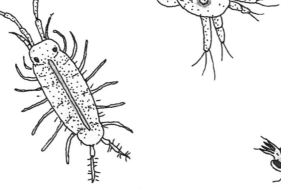

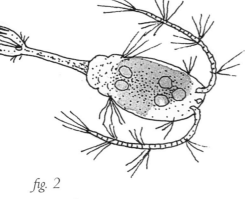

*fig. 2*
Copepods

*fig. 3*
Daphnia

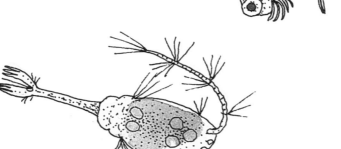

*fig. 4*
Opossum shrimps

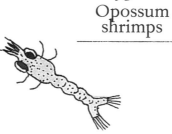

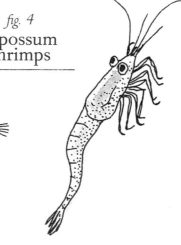

— *plate 17* —

# Ausubel's mighty claws lobster

*Dinochelus ausubeli*

Subphylum: CRUSTACEAN

This species of deep-sea lobster was
totally unknown until recently! Scientists
found it in the sea around the Philippines
in 2007, presenting their discovery in
2010. It is named after its elongated right-
hand claw and Jesse Ausubel, one of the
sponsors of the 2010 "Census of
Marine Life" (see Introduction).

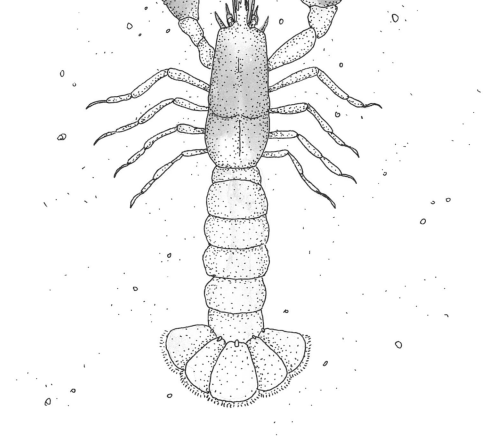

— *plate 18* —

Crabs are a large group of crustaceans with 3,500 species. They all have ten legs, and the front two have pincers. To find out if a crab is male or female, you must look at its abdomen: if it has three segments it is a male; if it has more than this, it is a female!

## Atlantic ghost crab

*Ocypode quadrata*

Subphylum: CRUSTACEAN

The ghost crab's name refers to the great speed at which it can hide itself by burrowing in the sand. One of its pincers is bigger than the other.

## Common shore crab

*Carcinus maenas*

Subphylum: CRUSTACEAN

This shoreline crab species is invasive. Originally from the North Atlantic coast it can now be found all over the world.

fig. 1

fig. 2

## Flower crab
(or blue crab, blue swimmer crab, sand crab)

*Portunus pelagicus*

Subphylum: CRUSTACEAN

This crab has velvety hairs on its shell and paddle-shaped back legs, which make it an excellent swimmer. The male is a brighter blue than the female.

fig. 3

— plate 19 —

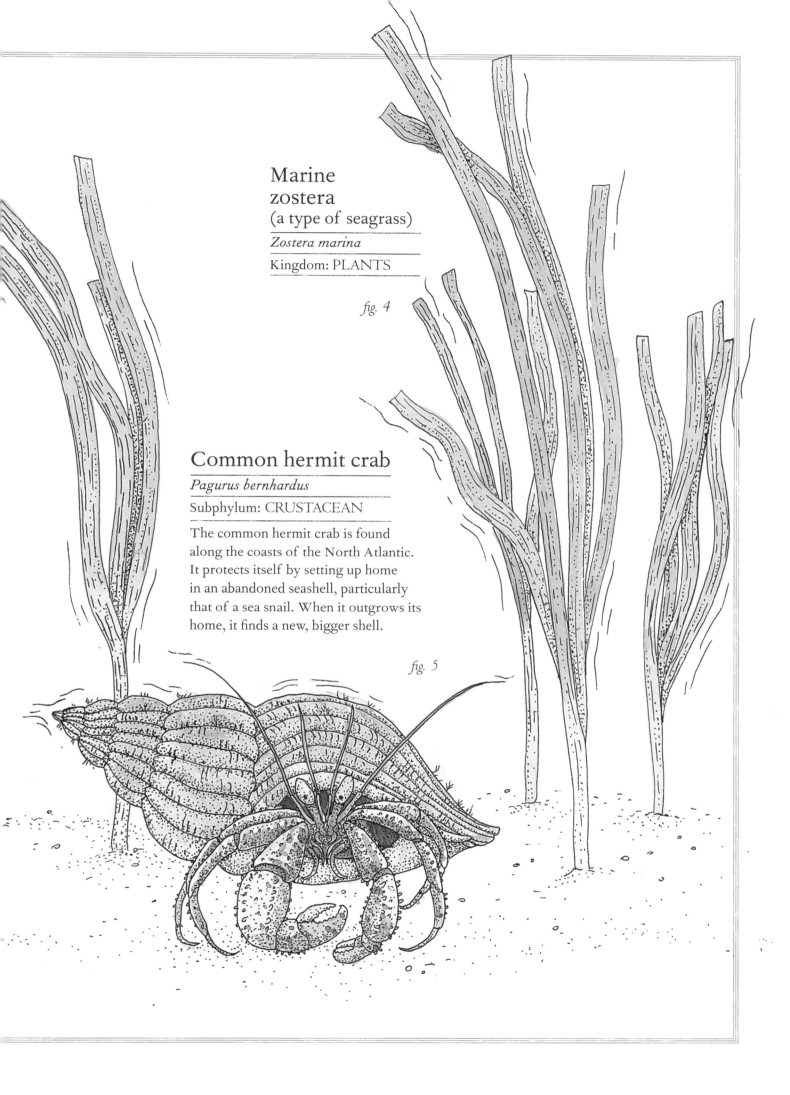

## Marine zostera
### (a type of seagrass)

*Zostera marina*

Kingdom: PLANTS

*fig. 4*

## Common hermit crab

*Pagurus bernhardus*

Subphylum: CRUSTACEAN

The common hermit crab is found along the coasts of the North Atlantic. It protects itself by setting up home in an abandoned seashell, particularly that of a sea snail. When it outgrows its home, it finds a new, bigger shell.

*fig. 5*

# Sponges

Sponges feed by filtering the seawater. They are not plants, despite their appearance, but animals with porous bodies that attach themselves to rocks.

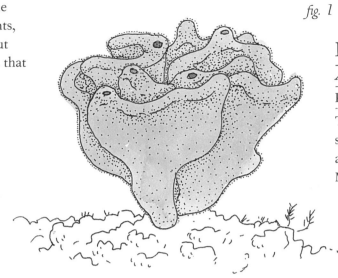

fig. 1

## Flat antlers sponge

*Axinella damicornis*

Phylum: PORIFERA

This velvety looking, yellow sponge lives in the calm and shallow waters of the Mediterranean Sea.

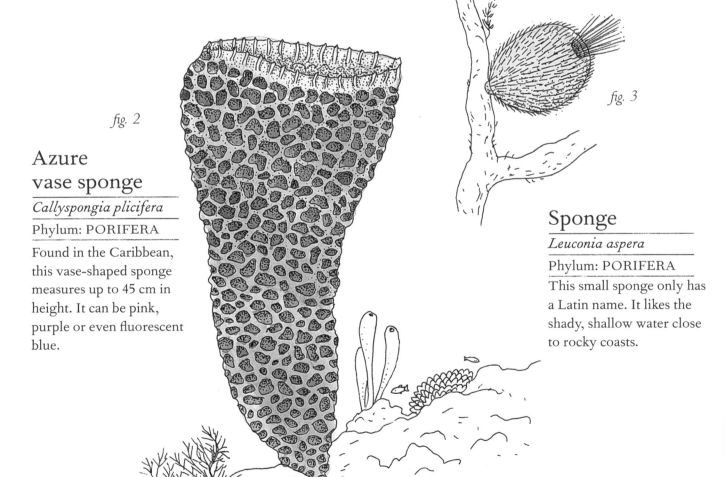

fig. 3

fig. 2

## Azure vase sponge

*Callyspongia plicifera*

Phylum: PORIFERA

Found in the Caribbean, this vase-shaped sponge measures up to 45 cm in height. It can be pink, purple or even fluorescent blue.

## Sponge

*Leuconia aspera*

Phylum: PORIFERA

This small sponge only has a Latin name. It likes the shady, shallow water close to rocky coasts.

— plate 20 —

# Breadcrumb sponge

*Halichondria panicea*

Phylum: PORIFERA

This sponge covers the rocks of shallow coastal waters, forming small "chimneys" about 1 to 3 cm high.

*fig. 4*

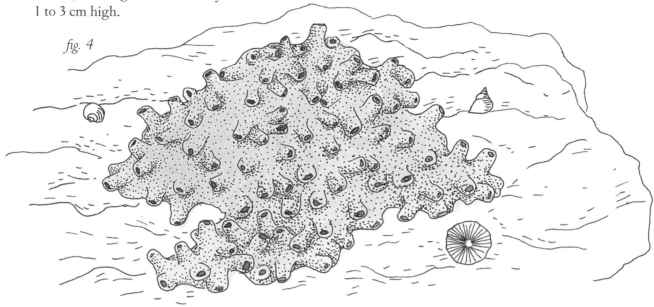

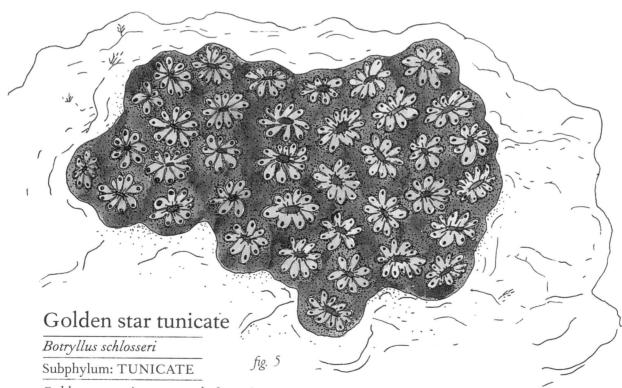

# Golden star tunicate

*Botryllus schlosseri*

Subphylum: TUNICATE

*fig. 5*

Golden star tunicates are only 3 mm in size but live together in a group or colony, creating a sponge-like effect. A tunicate is a completely different animal from a sponge.

These sea creatures are echinoderms. This word means "animal with a hedgehog skin". Many live in shallow seawater amongst marine plants. Starfish, shown on this plate, have suction cups on their arms which help them move around and open up the bivalve molluscs they eat.

## Common starfish

*Asterias rubens*

Class: ECHINODERM

*fig. 1*

## Starlet cushion starfish

*Asterina gibbosa*

Phylum: ECHINODERM

*fig. 2*

## Common sunstar

*Crossaster papposus*

Phylum: ECHINODERM

*fig. 3*

— *plate 21* —

## Mediterranean feather star

*fig. 1*

*Antedon mediterranea*

Phylum: ECHINODERM

This feather star has ten branched arms on which it catches its plankton food. It floats around the Mediterranean at depths of up to 80 m, occasionally attaching itself to other sea animals, such as sponges, or rocks.

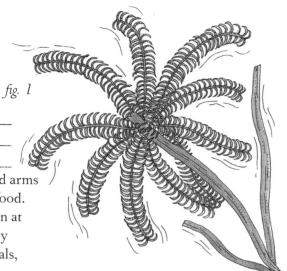

## Mediterranean tapeweed

*Posidonia oceanica*

Kingdom: PLANTS

Many sea plants are seaweed, a form of algae. This seagrass is not. It is a flowering plant, producing fruit known as "sea olives".

*fig. 2*

## White spine sea cucumber

*Holothuria poli*

Phylum: ECHINODERM

Despite their name, sea cucumbers are animals that move over the sea bed on tiny feet with suction cups. This one is found in the Mediterranean.

*fig. 3*

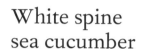

*fig. 4*

## Common caulerpa

*Caulerpa prolifera*

Class: GREEN ALGAE

*fig. 5*

## Kelp

*Laminaria*

Class: BROWN ALGAE

## Common sea urchin

*fig. 6*

*Echinus esculentus*

Phylum: ECHINODERM

The exoskeleton of the sea urchin, called a test, is covered with hundreds of mobile spikes. It uses them to protect itself from enemies, to move around the sea bed or to bury itself in the sand. The sea urchin grazes on seaweed such as kelp.

— *plate 22* —

# Smooth hammerhead shark

*Sphyrna zygaena*

Class: CARTILAGINOUS FISH

Cartilaginous fish, including sharks and rays, have skeletons made of flexible cartilage rather than bone. This shark has a flattened head, shaped like a hammer, with eyes at either end. It feeds on fish, crustaceans and squid.

— *plate 23* —

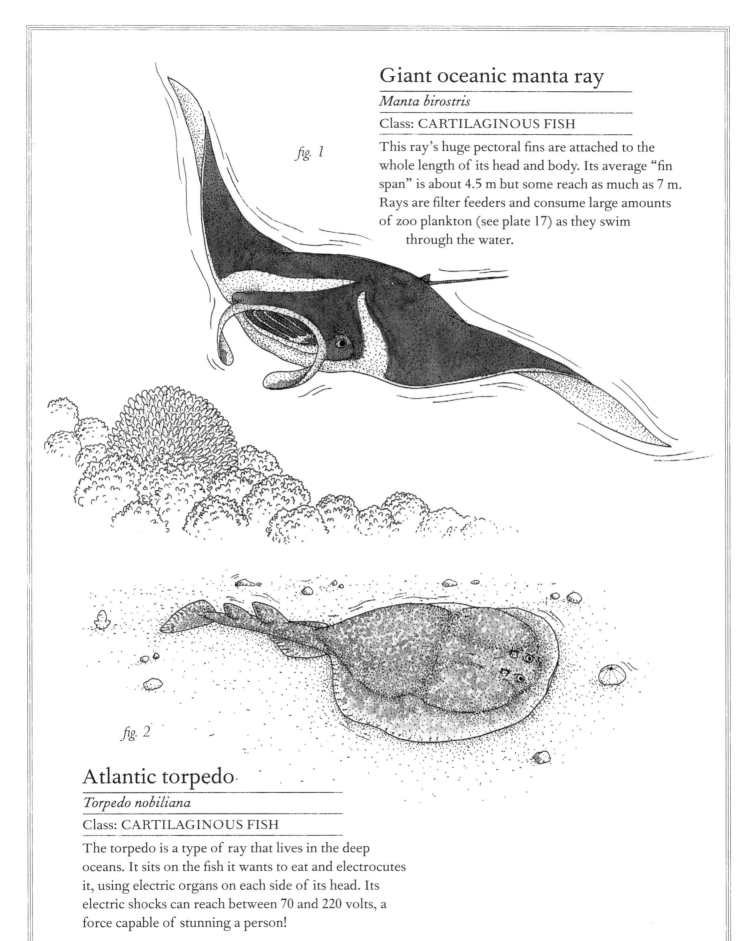

## Giant oceanic manta ray

*Manta birostris*

Class: CARTILAGINOUS FISH

This ray's huge pectoral fins are attached to the whole length of its head and body. Its average "fin span" is about 4.5 m but some reach as much as 7 m. Rays are filter feeders and consume large amounts of zoo plankton (see plate 17) as they swim through the water.

*fig. 1*

*fig. 2*

## Atlantic torpedo

*Torpedo nobiliana*

Class: CARTILAGINOUS FISH

The torpedo is a type of ray that lives in the deep oceans. It sits on the fish it wants to eat and electrocutes it, using electric organs on each side of its head. Its electric shocks can reach between 70 and 220 volts, a force capable of stunning a person!

— *plate 24* —

# Atlantic sailfish

*Istiophorus albicans*

Class: RAY-FINNED FISH

Most fish species are ray-finned, with skeletons
made of bone like mammals and reptiles. This
midnight blue ray-finned fish is 2 m long and has
a very pointed upper jaw, much like the swordfish.
It uses its dorsal fin, in the shape of a sail, to
jump out of the water. Capable of speeds up to
110 km/h, it is the fastest fish in the oceans.

— *plate 25* —

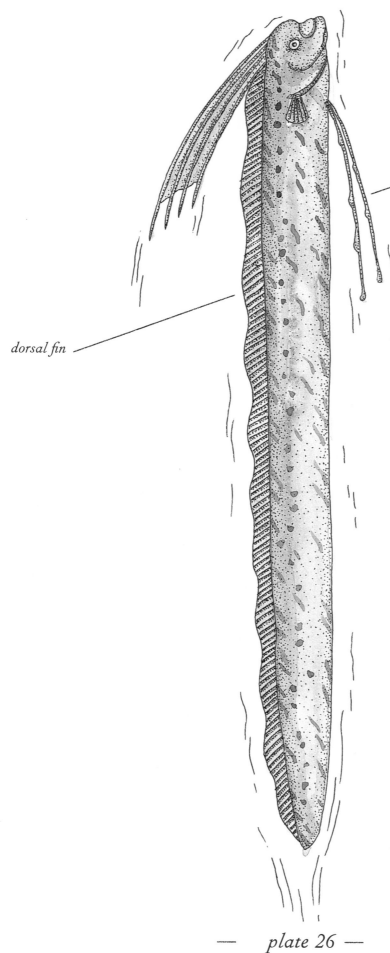

*pelvic fins*

*dorsal fin*

# Giant oarfish
## (or king of herrings)

*Regalecus glesne*

Class: RAY-FINNED FISH

Measuring as much as 11 m in length, the giant oarfish is the longest of all the bony fish. At the start of its bright red dorsal fin, there is a crest section, while its long pelvic fins look like oars, giving it its name. The oarfish sometimes holds itself vertically in the water and swims rather like an undulating snake, possibly inspiring the many "sea serpent" legends.

— *plate 26* —

# Atlantic salmon

*Salmo salar*

Class: RAY-FINNED FISH

The Atlantic salmon has red and blue stripes at the start of its life in a freshwater river. As it matures, these grow darker and its body more silvery. After about one to four years, the salmon travels down the river and into the sea, where it lives and grows (to lengths of about 73 cm) for another few years. It returns to the river where it started its life in order to lay eggs and die.

— *plate 27* —

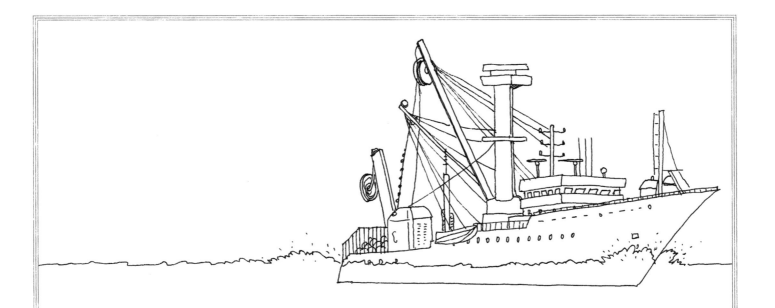

## Atlantic bluefin tuna

*Thunnus thynnus*

Class: RAY-FINNED FISH

This fast predator can measure up to 4.5 m and weighs more than 650 kg! People love to eat this type of tuna, particularly in Japan. As a result it has been heavily overfished and is now an endangered species.

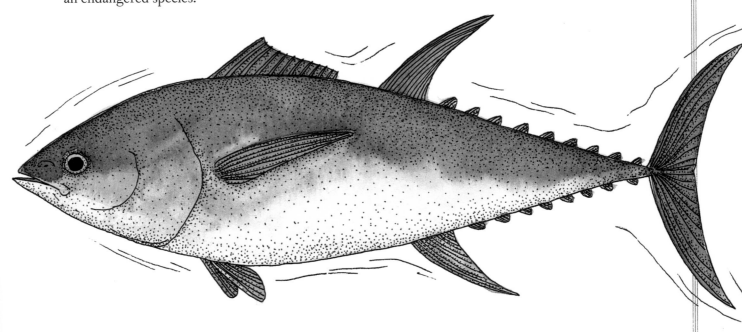

— *plate 28* —

# European pilchard or sardine

*Sardina pilchardus*

Class: RAY-FINNED FISH

These small fish are very good swimmers and live in groups called schools. These are made up of thousands of sardines all of the same age. In the Mediterranean, fishermen use a light in order to attract and capture sardines at night.

*fig. 1*

*fig. 2*

# Atlantic mackerel

*Scomber scombrus*

Class: RAY-FINNED FISH

Mackerel move together in large schools, staying in deep water in the winter but coming closer to the coast in spring to feed on prawns and small fish during the summer.

— *plate 29* —

# Long snouted seahorse

*Hippocampus guttulatus*

Class: RAY-FINNED FISH

Despite its horse-like head this is a fish, with gills to breathe. Its tail rolls up so it can attach itself to seaweed. After the female lays her eggs, the male fertilises them and then carries them in a pouch on his stomach until they hatch.

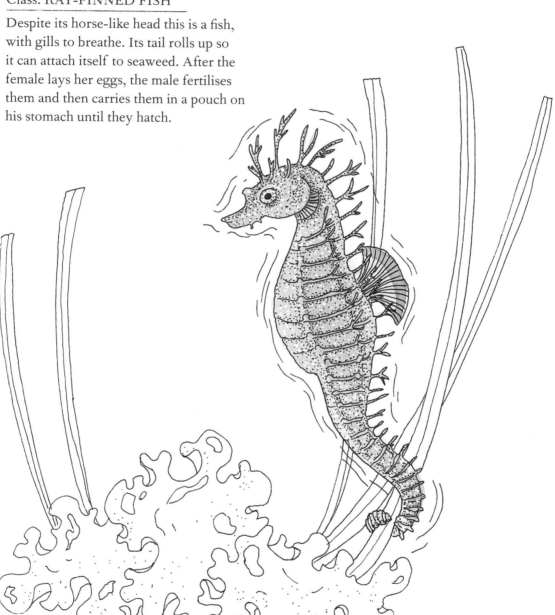

— *plate 30* —

# Turkey moray eel

*Gymnothorax meleagris*

Class: RAY-FINNED FISH

This Pacific fish can reach 1.2 m in length.
It lives in shallow water coral reefs where
its brown colour and white spots help to
camouflage it.

— *plate 31* —

# Lionfish

*Pterois miles*

Class: RAY-FINNED FISH

Found in the coral reefs of the Pacific and Indian oceans, this fish uses its wide lower fins to push its prey into a corner before drawing it into its large mouth. It is protected by highly venomous stings in its dorsal fin, powerful enough to kill a human.

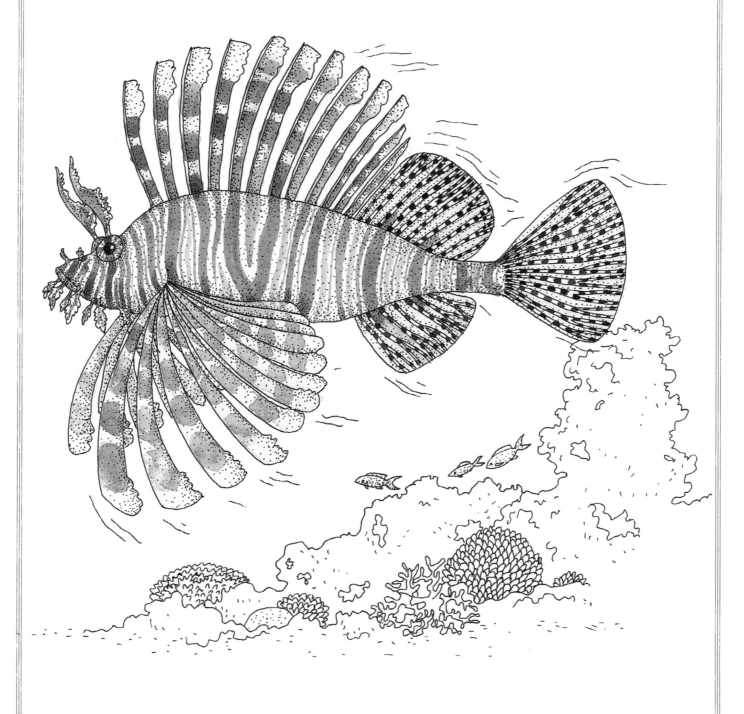

— *plate 32* —

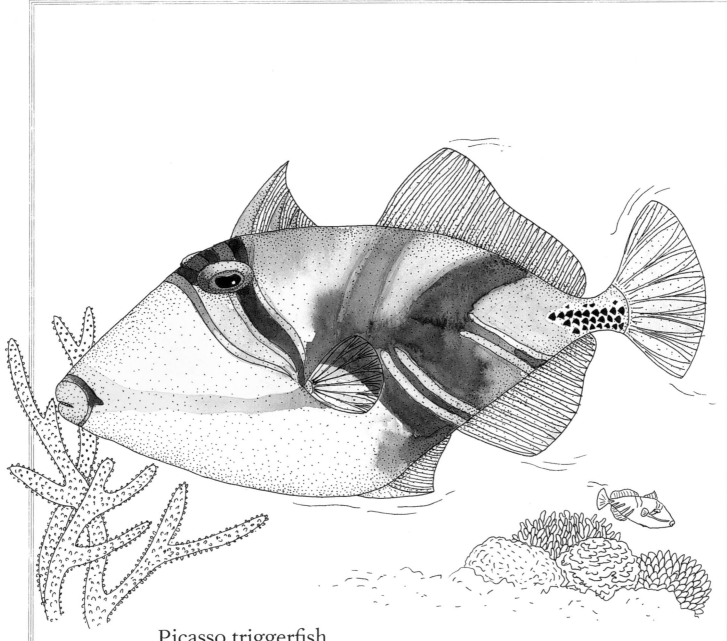

## Picasso triggerfish

*Rhinecanthus aculeatus*

Class: RAY-FINNED FISH

The bright colours and angular shape of this fish
bring to mind Picasso's paintings, hence its name.
Like all triggerfish, it has three prickly spines on
its back which usually lie flat but it can erect them
suddenly (like pulling a trigger) as a means of
defence. These fish live in the coral reefs of the
Indian and Pacific oceans. They are territorial and
will attack intruders who stray into their patch.
They also make strange sounds when lifted out of
the water.

— *plate 33* —

# Red Sea bannerfish

*Heniochus intermedius*

Class: RAY-FINNED FISH

This fish has an elongated dorsal fin. Found in the Red Sea and the Gulf, it is a species of butterflyfish, small sea fish of the coral reefs. These fish mainly live alone as adults but come together for a while each year to mate, always choosing the same partner.

— *plate 34* —

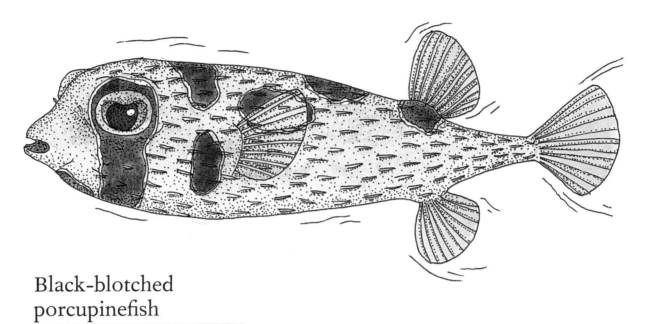

# Black-blotched porcupinefish

*Diodon liturosus*

Class: RAY-FINNED FISH

Found in the coral and rocky reefs of the Indian and Pacific oceans, this fish triples in size as a means of defence. It swallows lots of water when disturbed and swells up, pushing out poisonous spikes.

— *plate 35* —

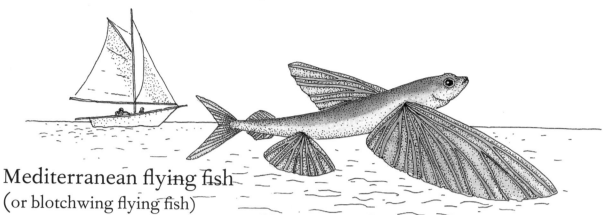

## Mediterranean flying fish
## (or blotchwing flying fish)

*Cheilopogon heterurus*

Class: RAY-FINNED FISH

This fish does not fly but glides over the water, using its four highly-developed pectoral fins. It is capable of jumping 1 m above the surface of the water and can travel through the air for 200 m.

*fig. 1*

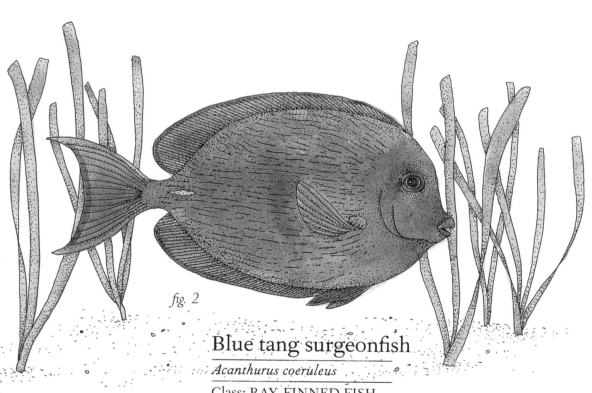

*fig. 2*

*fig. 3*

## Turtlegrass

*Thalassia testudinum*

Kingdom: PLANTS

## Blue tang surgeonfish

*Acanthurus coeruleus*

Class: RAY-FINNED FISH

Found in Atlantic coral reefs, this fish changes colour as it grows: it is yellow when young, then yellow and blue and goes completely blue as an adult, reaching about 35 cm in size. It gets the name "surgeonfish" because of blades on its tail that stand up when it is threatened. They are a defence mechanism and are not used to attack, as the fish only eats seaweed.

— *plate 36* —

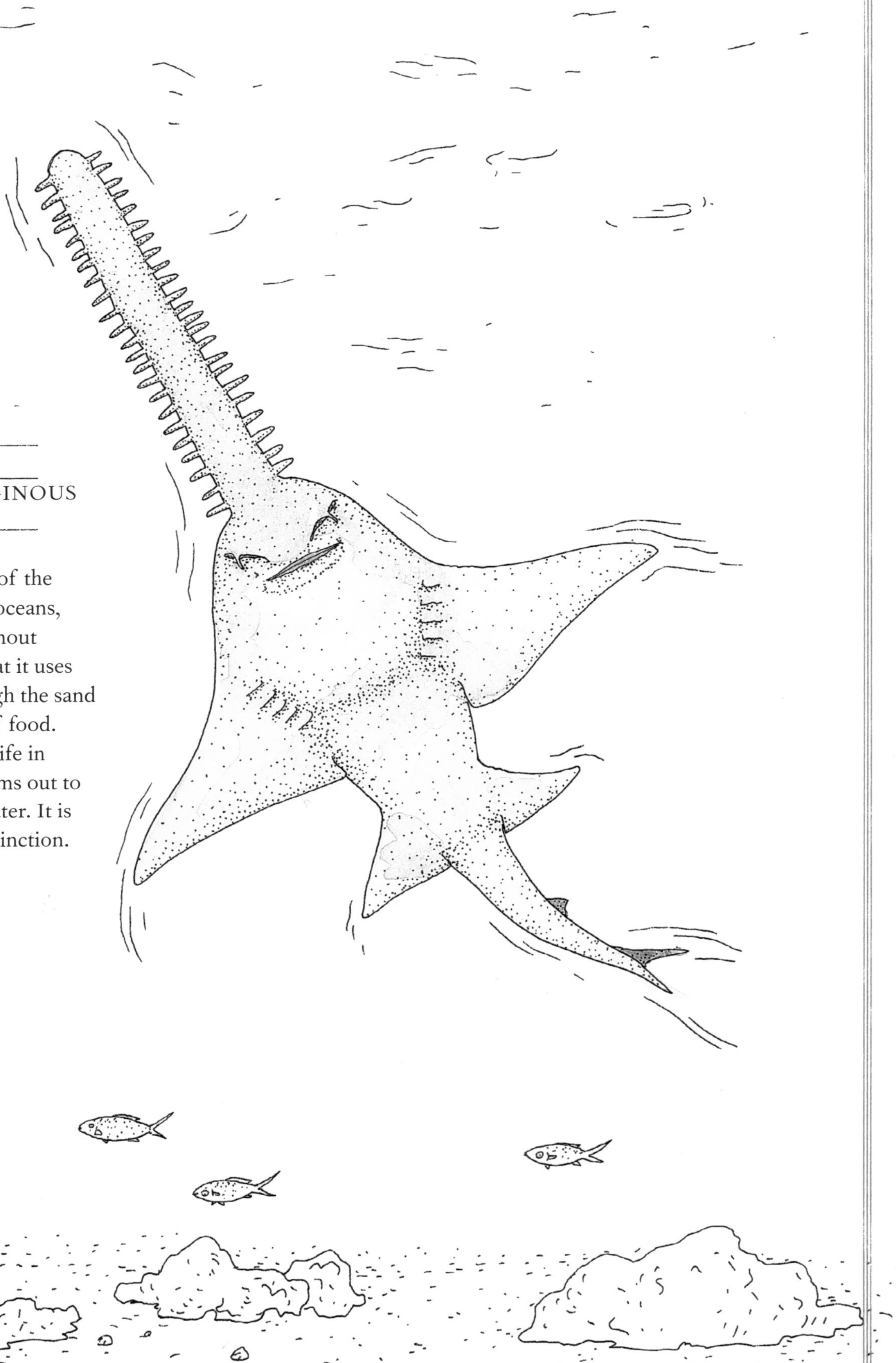

# Largetooth sawfish

*Pristis microdon*

Class: CARTILAGINOUS FISH

This fish, from the subtropical waters of the Indian and Pacific oceans, has a saw-shaped snout covered in teeth that it uses to rummage through the sand and silt in search of food. The sawfish starts life in freshwater and swims out to sea a few months later. It is threatened with extinction.

*— plate 37 —*

# Longnose butterflyfish
## (or big longnose butterflyfish)

*Forcipiger longirostris*

Class: RAY-FINNED FISH

The long jaws that give this fish its name allow it to search for prey in the nooks and crannies of the coral reefs beyond the reach of other fish.

*fig. 1*

# Queen angelfish

*Holacanthus ciliaris*

Class: RAY-FINNED FISH

This yellow and blue fish from the reefs of the western Atlantic has long, pointed back fins. Like all angelfish, it has a spike on each side of its head, forming part of its gill covers.

*fig. 2*

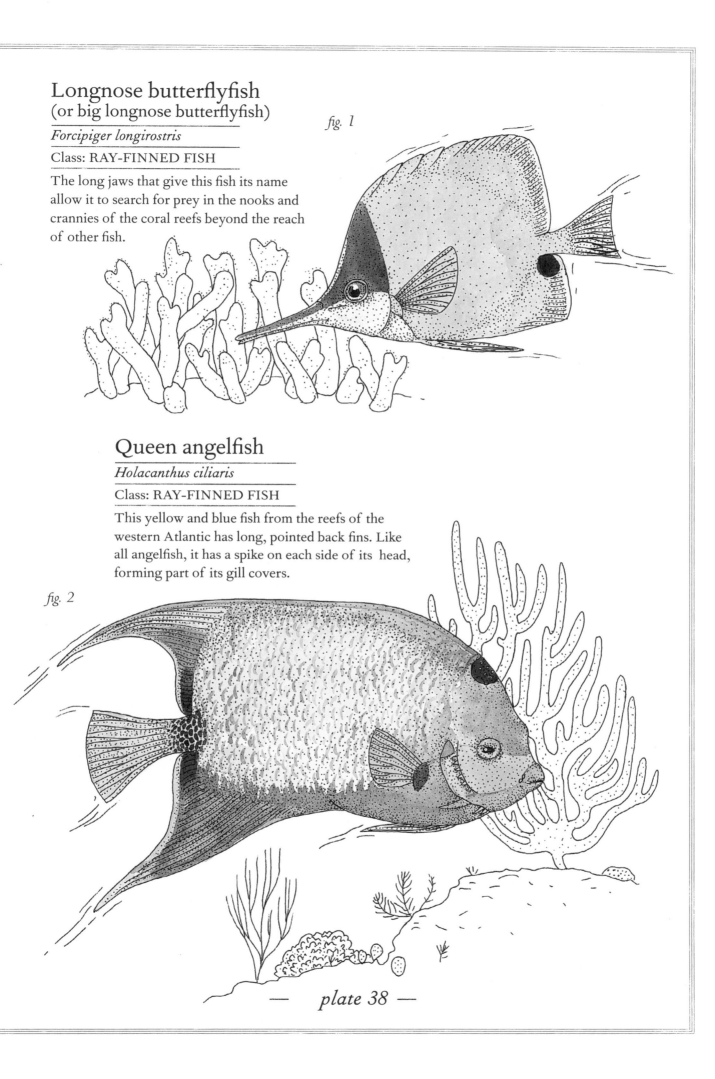

— *plate 38* —

# Viperfish

*Chauliodus*

Class: RAY-FINNED FISH

This type of fish lives in the deep ocean where it is very dark. It has such long teeth in its jaw that it cannot close its mouth. It has two parallel rows of light-giving organs on its stomach and at the end of the long spine on its dorsal fin. It flashes these light organs on and off to lure its prey and to attract a mate.

— *plate 39* —

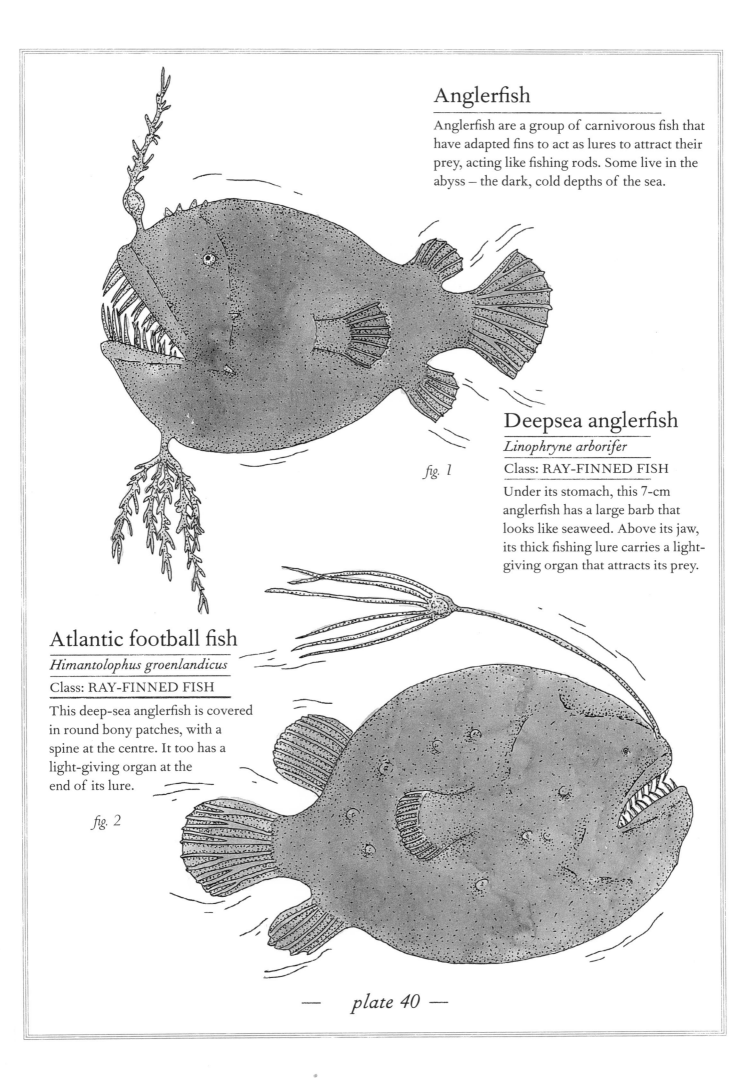

# Anglerfish

Anglerfish are a group of carnivorous fish that have adapted fins to act as lures to attract their prey, acting like fishing rods. Some live in the abyss – the dark, cold depths of the sea.

*fig. 1*

## Deepsea anglerfish

*Linophryne arborifer*

Class: RAY-FINNED FISH

Under its stomach, this 7-cm anglerfish has a large barb that looks like seaweed. Above its jaw, its thick fishing lure carries a light-giving organ that attracts its prey.

## Atlantic football fish

*Himantolophus groenlandicus*

Class: RAY-FINNED FISH

This deep-sea anglerfish is covered in round bony patches, with a spine at the centre. It too has a light-giving organ at the end of its lure.

*fig. 2*

— *plate 40* —

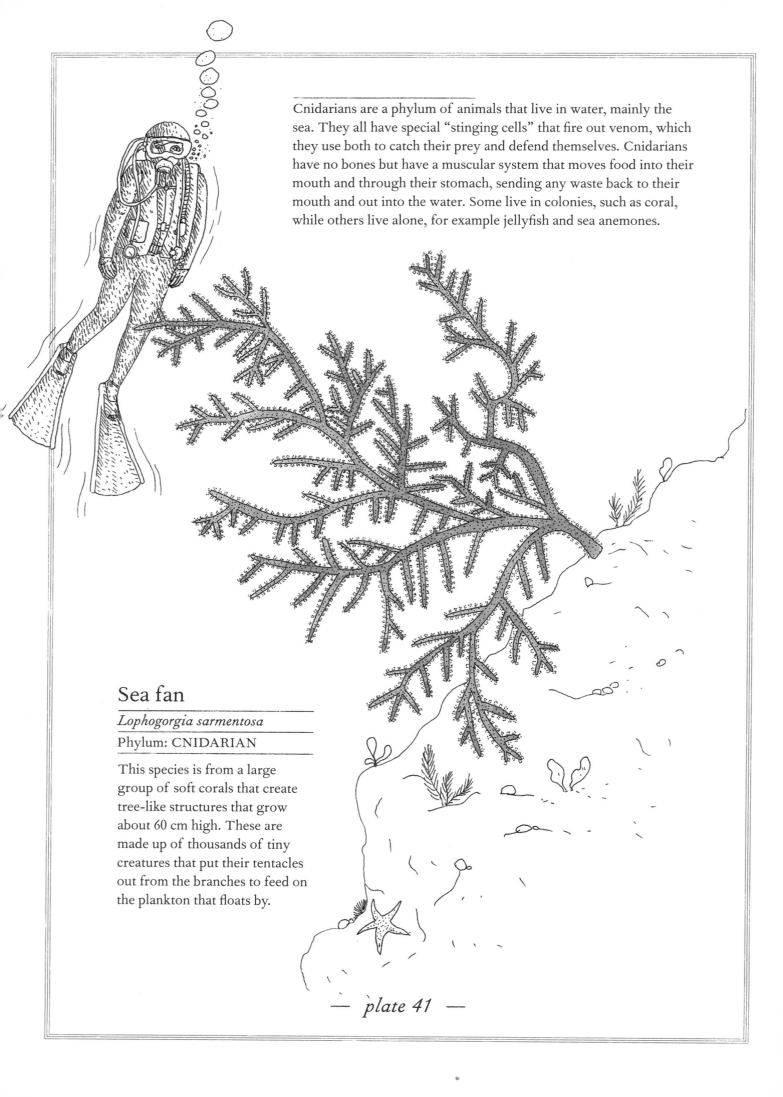

Cnidarians are a phylum of animals that live in water, mainly the sea. They all have special "stinging cells" that fire out venom, which they use both to catch their prey and defend themselves. Cnidarians have no bones but have a muscular system that moves food into their mouth and through their stomach, sending any waste back to their mouth and out into the water. Some live in colonies, such as coral, while others live alone, for example jellyfish and sea anemones.

# Sea fan

*Lophogorgia sarmentosa*

Phylum: CNIDARIAN

This species is from a large group of soft corals that create tree-like structures that grow about 60 cm high. These are made up of thousands of tiny creatures that put their tentacles out from the branches to feed on the plankton that floats by.

— *plate 41* —

## Sea pen

*Pennatula*

Phylum: CNIDARIAN

The colonies of this group of
soft corals have a quill-pen shape,
that gives them their name.

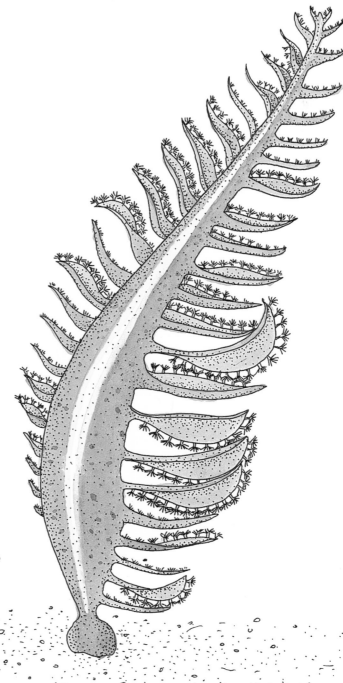

— *plate 42* —

# Grooved-brain coral

## *Diploria labyrinthiformis*

Class: CNIDARIAN

This brain-shaped cnidarian colony produces some of the hard structures that help build coral reefs. It is found in warmer waters in the western Atlantic Ocean.

— *plate 43* —

## False percula clownfish

*Amphiprion ocellaris*

Class: BONY FISH

The clownfish lives among the magnificent sea anemone's tentacles, protected from their sting by mucus that covers its body. Predators leave the clownfish alone to avoid the anemone's sting, while the fish's leftovers provide its host with food.

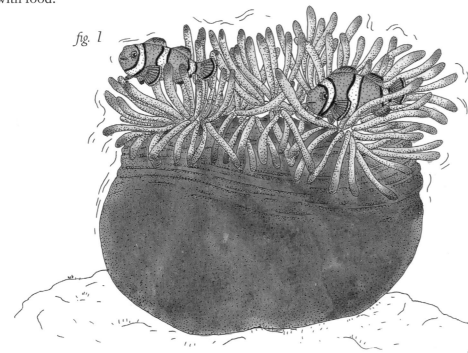

*fig. 1*

*fig. 2*

## Magnificent sea anemone

*Heteractis magnifica*

Class: CNIDARIAN

The stinging tentacles of this large sea anemone can be 8 cm long.

*fig. 3*

## Mauve stinger

*Pelagia noctiluca*

Class: CNIDARIAN

This species of jellyfish has stinging cells all over its body. Its venomous stings paralyse its prey before it swallows it. Mauve stingers glow in the dark.

— *plate 44* —

# Marine iguana

*Amblyrhynchus cristatus*

Class: REPTILE

This reptile from the Galapagos Islands is the only lizard that lives mainly in the sea. It swims through the water using its tail, diving under the surface to feed on seaweed. Once back on land, it filters out the salt it has swallowed through its nose, spraying it out of its nostrils in a jet of mucus.

fig. 1

fig. 2

# Sea lettuce

*Ulva*

Kingdom: PLANTS

— *plate 45* —

# Saltwater crocodile

*Crocodylus porosus*

Class: REPTILE

This crocodile is a very dangerous giant, measuring 6 m in length and preying on other large animals, including humans. It lives in the estuaries and mangrove swamps of south-east Asia and Australia. The female lays her eggs in a nest, which she guards until they hatch. She carries the hatchlings to the water in her mouth and remains with them for several months.

— plate 46 —

# Green sea turtle

*Chelonia mydas*

Class: REPTILE ·

The green sea turtle has a smooth, olive-brown shell and lives in warmer coastal waters. It is named after its green-coloured flesh, which is caused by its herbivorous diet – it eats large quantities of seagrass and seaweed. As a reptile, a sea turtle needs to come to the surface to breathe but can stay underwater for several hours, even sleeping when submerged. The turtles return to land to lay their eggs and, unlike other sea turtle species, to bask in the sun.

— *plate 47* —

## Calcareous tubeworm

*Serpula vermicularis*

Phylum: WORM

This worm lives in a chalky tube
attached to a rock. At high tide, it
pokes out its red feelers to feed on
plankton; at low tide, it closes up
again, sealing its tube with a trumpet-
shaped lid at the centre of its feelers.

*fig. 1*

## Lugworm

*Arenicola marina*

Phylum: WORM

This 10- to 25-cm red worm digs a U-shaped tunnel
in the sand or the silt. There can be as many as a 100
to 150 worms in square metre of beach. The lugworm
eats its way through the sand, extracting its food,
the plant particles and tiny animals that live in it. It
excretes or poos out the waste sand in worm-shaped
piles which you can often see on the beach at low tide.

## Ragworm

*Hediste diversicolor*

Phylum: WORM

This 10-cm worm lives in the
sand and spins a mucus net
outside its burrow to catch its
plankton food. It also comes
out to hunt for larger prey.

*fig. 3*

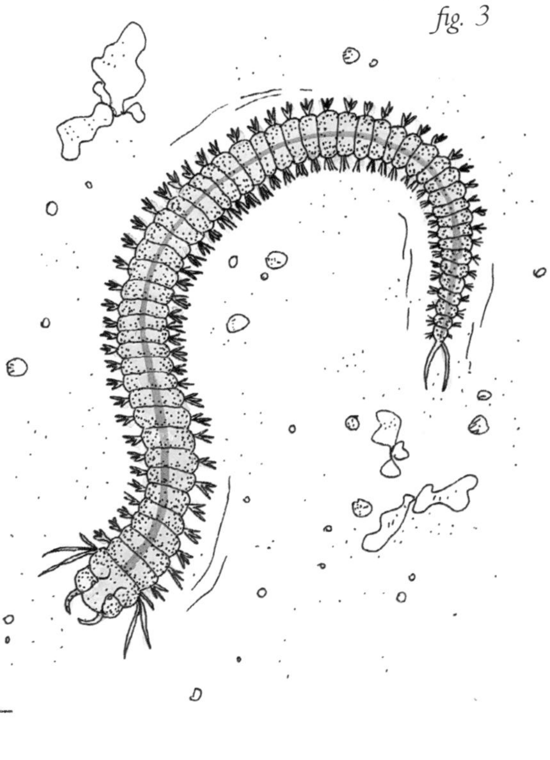

*fig. 2*

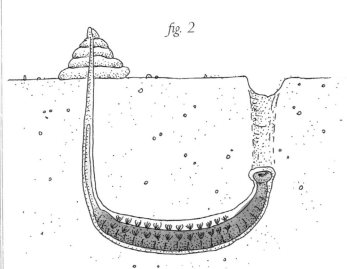

— *plate 48* —

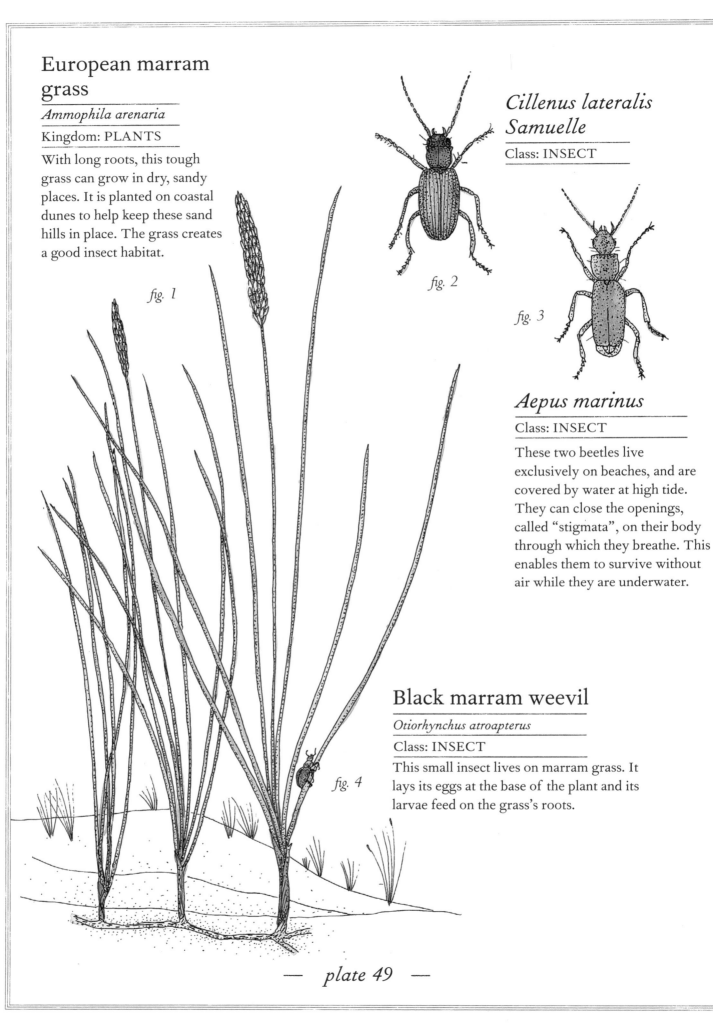

# European marram grass

*Ammophila arenaria*

Kingdom: PLANTS

With long roots, this tough grass can grow in dry, sandy places. It is planted on coastal dunes to help keep these sand hills in place. The grass creates a good insect habitat.

*fig. 1*

# *Cillenus lateralis Samuelle*

Class: INSECT

*fig. 2*

*fig. 3*

# *Aepus marinus*

Class: INSECT

These two beetles live exclusively on beaches, and are covered by water at high tide. They can close the openings, called "stigmata", on their body through which they breathe. This enables them to survive without air while they are underwater.

# Black marram weevil

*Otiorhynchus atroapterus*

Class: INSECT

This small insect lives on marram grass. It lays its eggs at the base of the plant and its larvae feed on the grass's roots.

*fig. 4*

— *plate 49* —

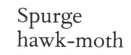

# Spurge hawk-moth

*Hyles euphorbiae*

Class: INSECT

*fig. 5*

This moth lays its eggs on sea spurge. Its larvae feed on the plant when they hatch.

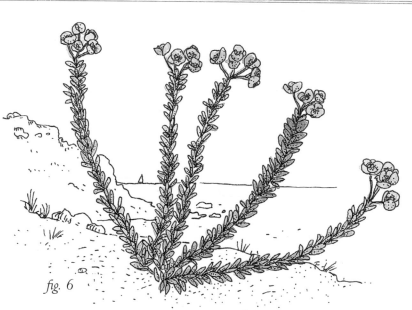

*fig. 6*

# Sea spurge

*Euphorbia paralias*

Kingdom: PLANTS

This spurge grows on sandy coasts, often close to colonies of nesting birds. It flowers from May to September.

*fig. 7*

# Mining bee

*Andrena vaga*

Class: INSECT

The mining bee digs a hole in sandy soils to make a nest for her eggs and young.

*fig. 8*

# Red-banded sand wasp

*Ammophila sabulosa*

Class: INSECT

This wasp feeds on the nectar from flowers, but its larvae are carnivorous! The wasp makes burrows in the sand then puts a caterpillar in each burrow, which it has paralysed with its sting. The wasp then lays an egg in each burrow. When the egg hatches, the larva has a caterpillar to feed on!

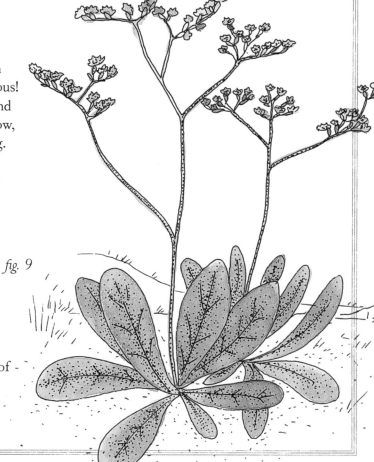

*fig. 9*

# Common sea lavender

*Limonium vulgare*

Kingdom: PLANTS

This plant grows along the sandy coasts of the Atlantic and the Mediterranean.

# Atlantic puffin

*Fratercula arctica*

Class: BIRD

This bird spends most of its life out at sea, only returning to land to nest in burrows on grassy cliffs in the spring. It can dive to depths of 15 m under the water to catch small fish that it swallows immediately or crams into its beak in order to bring them to its chick (called a puffling!). Its webbed feet act like rudders under the water.

— *plate 50* —

## Southern royal albatross

*Diomedea epomophora*

Class: BIRD

With its 3-m wingspan, this bird rivals
the wandering albatross for the title
of largest seabird. Like all species of
albatross, it flies over the oceans of the
southern hemisphere. The albatross
mates for life, returning to the same
partner to breed once a year.

— *plate 51* —

# Emperor penguin

*Aptenodytes forsteri*

Class: BIRD

The penguin cannot fly but its wings are
perfectly adapted to underwater swimming,
acting like fins. The emperor penguin can dive
to depths of over 400 m. On land it stands
upright, living in colonies on the frozen lands
of Antarctica.

— *plate 52* —

# Razorbills

*Alca torda*

Class: BIRD

These birds are related to puffins and follow a similar lifestyle, spending much of their time out over the waters of the North Atlantic. The birds mate for life, nesting in colonies on cliffs and raising one chick per year. The parents share "chick" care, taking it in turns to sit on the egg and feed the chick when it hatches.

— *plate 53* —

# Great black-backed gull

*Larus marinus*

Class: BIRD

This large, North Atlantic gull eats just about anything. It looks for fish and crustaceans along the coast and in the sea but can also be found inland feeding on scraps on rubbish tips. It will steal chicks from other birds' nests and will even hunt adult birds.

*fig. 1*

*fig. 2*

# Oystercatcher

*Haematopus ostralegus*

Class: BIRD

This wading bird lives along coasts and estuaries, looking for food along the water's edge. An oystercatcher's beak is well adapted for finding the bivalves it likes to eat buried in the sand and for opening their shells. The birds mate for life and nest away from the shore, sometimes quite far inland.

— *plate 54* —

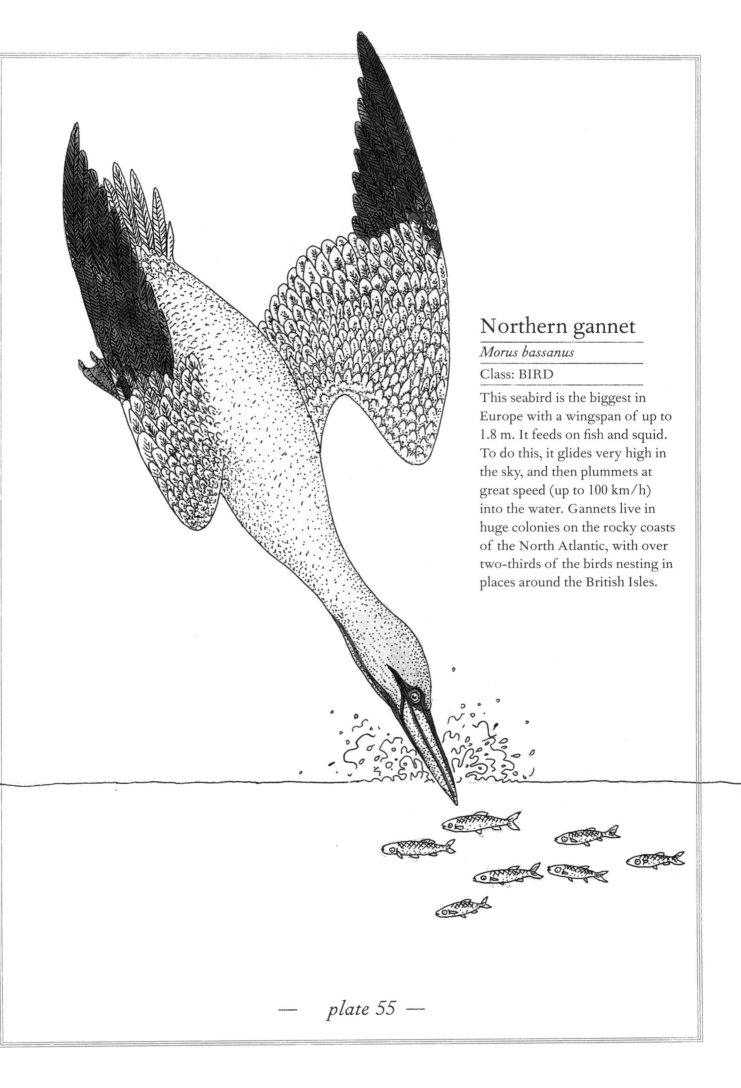

# Northern gannet

*Morus bassanus*

Class: BIRD

This seabird is the biggest in Europe with a wingspan of up to 1.8 m. It feeds on fish and squid. To do this, it glides very high in the sky, and then plummets at great speed (up to 100 km/h) into the water. Gannets live in huge colonies on the rocky coasts of the North Atlantic, with over two-thirds of the birds nesting in places around the British Isles.

— *plate 55* —

# GLOSSARY

*algae* Simple life forms that grow in or near water.

*animal* A living creature, such as a bird, insect, fish, reptile, insect or mammal, including a human, that has to eat food for its energy.

*Antarctic* The southern area of the Earth near the South Pole.

*Arctic* The northern area of the Earth near the North Pole.

*baleen plates* Flexible, comb-like structures, which hang from the upper jaw of certain whales. They sieve the whales' food from the water.

*bird* A class of animals covered with feathers that has wings and two feet and can usually fly.

*bivalve* A class of mollusc, such as a mussel or an oyster, that has a shell in two parts.

*breathe* In an animal, to take air in and out of the lungs or, underwater, through the gills.

*breed* In animals, sexual reproduction to produce young.

*camouflage* Colour, pattern or shape that allows an object or animal to blend into the background and not be noticed.

*carnivore* An animal that eats mainly meat.

*cartilaginous fish* A class of fish, including sharks and rays, that have skeletons formed of cartilage rather than bone.

*cephalopod* A class of animals, including octopus, squid and cuttlefish, that has tentacles and swims by pushing water out of its body.

*class* In classification, a large group of living things with similar characteristics.

*classification* In science, the organisation of different living things into categories, starting with a kingdom (such as animals) then breaking this down into smaller and smaller groups.

*climate change* A change in world climate, the usual weather and temperature of a place, particularly in the past 50 years.

*cnidarian* One of the cnidaria phylum, a large group of animals with a sting (about 9,000) such as jellyfish.

*compendium* A collection of information presented clearly but in few words.

*coral reef* A solid underwater structure made up of the skeletons of tiny animals called corals.

*crustacean* A subphylum of animals with a soft body divided into sections and a hard outer shell. Most live in water, including crabs.

*dinosaur* One of an extinct group of reptiles that lived on Earth millions of years ago.

*dorsal fin* A fin on the back of many marine animals that helps to keep their position in the water, and prevent them from rolling over.

*echinoderm* A phylum of marine animals, such as a starfish or a sea star. Echinoderms often have spiny skin and have a symmetrical body shape.

*ecosystem* All the living things – animals and plants – that live together in a particular place.

*extinction* When a species dies out completely.

*fertilise* In animals, when a female egg joins with male sperm to start developing a new animal.

*gastropod* A large and diverse class of molluscs. Snails and slugs are gastropods.

*gills* The body organ that fish (and the young of some amphibians) use to breathe.

*gland* An organ in an animal's body that produces hormones or makes saliva or tears.

*habitat* The natural home or environment where an animal or a plant usually lives.

*herbivore* An animal that eats only plants.

*insect* A class of animals with six legs, a three-sectioned body, no backbone and often wings.

*invasive* Fast spreading.

*invertebrates* animals without backbones.

*kingdom* In the classification system, one of the five big groups of living things on Earth including animals and plants.

*larva* The stage in the lifecycle of some animals after it hatches from an egg and before it develops into an adult.

*lure* A dangling structure that some fish use to attract and capture prey.

*mammal* A class of animals that have warm blood, hair or fur. Most give birth to live young and the mothers produce milk to feed them.

*marine* Of the sea.

*mate* The sexual partner of an animal. Used as a verb, it is the sexual act that forms part of animal reproduction.

*mollusc* A large phylum of animals that often has a shell and a muscular foot, including slugs, snails and octopuses.

*mucus* A thick, sticky fluid.

*organ* A body structure with a specific function, such as the heart, stomach or brain.

*pelvic fin* One of a pair of fins on the underside of the body of a fish.

*phylum* In classification, the group that comes beneath a kingdom and above a class or subphylum.

*pigment* A natural colour occurring in an animal or a plant.

*plankton* A very small animal or plant that lives in water, floating freely with its currents.

*plant* A living thing that grows in soil, water or on another plant and generally makes its own food energy.

*predator* An animal that hunts other animals for food.

*prey* An animal that is hunted and killed for food by another.

*ray-finned fish* A large and diverse class of fish that are named by their fins, which are formed from bony structures with skin covering them.

*reptile* A class of animals that have a backbone and are usually cold-blooded, with scaly skin.

*school* A large number of fish that swim and live together.

*species* A group of animals that can breed together to produce fertile offspring.

*sponge (porifera)* A phylum of simple marine animals which attach themselves to something solid on the sea bed, filtering food out of water.

*subphylum* In classification, a category below phylum and above class.

*siphon* A tube structure in the body of some molluscs, such as squid and mussels, used to bring water in and out of the body.

*tentacle* One of the long, flexible arms of an octopus or other animal.

*tide* The rising and falling of the sea, usually twice a day, as a result of the pull of gravity from the Sun and the Moon.

*venomous* Able to poison another animal.

*wingspan* The total measurement from tip to tip of a bird's wings when they are outstretched.

*worm* A creeping or crawling animal. In this instance, refers to the animals in the annelid phylum of animals.

# INDEX OF PLATES